Mick's 365 Writing Prompts

ISBN: 9781791396084

I have found professional writing success in spinning up ideas from prompts, random word lists, photos, bible passages, poems, quotes - almost anything.

This reference book is filled with 365 writing prompts to keep your mental juices percolating for a year (or more). Use them as-is, or allow your mind to wander over the mental pictures they conjure; I bet you'll be surprised where you end up!

Go forth and be fruitful, dear writer.

-Mickey Kulp, S.D.G.
Atlanta, GA, January 2019

1. Write a detailed description of a pet, past or present. Include looks and behaviors.

2. Write about the nearest tree.

3. Write something that comes to mind after reading this: "May your trails be crooked, winding, lonesome, dangerous, leading to the most amazing view. May your mountains rise into and above the clouds." -Edward Abbey

4. Write about a storm from a squirrel's perspective.

5. Write a letter to a fictional character.

6. Write about a character's first funeral.

7. Write a set of three haiku about: your shoes, cold water, and cotton candy.

8. Write a diaper commercial featuring your favorite fictional villian.

9. Write about a most memorable time at a sporting event.

10. Write about the last time you cried.

11. Write about a character finding a half-charred photo on the street dated 25 years ago.

12. Write about a character secretly watching a guy in a hoodie spray paint on a wall.

13. Write about a toddler chasing bubbles.

14. Write about the worst boss in the world.

15. Write about a girl that befriends a fairy in her backyard.

16. Write about a door that won't open.

17. Write about a character's secret superpower.

18. Write about a character helping a deaf person to cook their favorite meal.

19. Write about a character washing their car before giving to a loved one.

20. Write about a character being the only one small enough to rescue a dog from a storm drain.

21. Write about a character waking up in a strange place.

22. Write about a character singing in front of 20,000 people at a concert.

23. Write about a character's first day in heaven.

24. Write about a character finding a tiny, intelligent robot in their jacket pocket.

25. Write about being the tallest person on earth.

26. Write about a character answering a phone call from the US president.

27. Write about a character's camping trip on Mars.

28. Write about meeting the Grim Reaper at the supermarket
cereal aisle.

29. Write about a character discovering they have a twin
sibling.

30. Write about a character getting a mangled letter dated 100
years in the future.

31. Write about a character waking from a dream and finding it
is true.

32. Write about a character on a cross-country road trip.

33. Write about a character going to get a haircut and
discovering their ex is the stylist.

34. Write about a character chasing an alpaca that stole their
phone.

35. Write about a character answering the doorbell and finding
Hitler dressed like a clown.

36. Write something that comes to mind after reading this:
"I said to my soul, be still, and wait without hope,
For hope would be hope for the wrong thing." -T. S. Eliot

37. Write about a character's child bringing home a stray
kitten, then realizing it is a skunk.

38. Write about something that is directly behind you.

39. Write about a pro wrestler and a nun discussing the best way to express a dog's anal glands.

40. Write about an elephant escaping from the zoo and appearing in a character's yard.

41. Write about a character standing on the roof of a car while flood waters rise around it.

42. Write about a character hiking in the woods and finding a coffin partially revealed in a mudslide.

43. Write about the waiting area in an emergency room.

44. Write about a character's ability to become invisible if they hold their breath.

45. Write about a character finding that his/her cat changes to a tiger for one hour after eating a piece of raw bacon.

46. Write about a character's day after a ghost announces they have 24 hours left to live.

47. Write about a character walking through a giant corn maze in Autumn.

48. Write about a character's blind date with a crime scene photographer.

49. Write about a character finding a compass that always points to someone needing help.

50. Write about a character seeing tiny words appear on the petals of a flower.

51. Write about a character waking up and discovering they are handcuffed to a Neanderthal.

52. Write about a nuclear-powered toothbrush.

53. Write about a character finding a barnacle-encrusted crate on the beach.

54. Write about a character who stayed on a small island while others fled the hurricane.

55. Write about a character quitting a job that they hate.

56. Write about a wild raccoon sitting on the hood of your character's car.

57. Write about a character presenting a controversial topic to a panel of sour business execs.

58. Write about a character's Alaskan dog sled adventure.

59. Write about a mean person who was unexpectedly nice.

60. Write about the last bird left on earth.

61. Write about a character shrinking to the size of a flea.

62. Write about what happens after a genie offers a character three wishes.

63. Write about a character surfacing from a scuba dive and finding the boat has vanished.

64. Write about a postal carrier in a town of fifty people.

65. Write about a day in the life of a character in 1778.

66. Write something that comes to mind after reading this: "I guess the definition of a lunatic is a man surrounded by them." -Ezra Pound

67. Write about a character discovering that their departed grandmother was once a CIA analyst.

68. Write about a character reading an old book and discovering that the main plot points match their life exactly. Do they continue reading ahead?

69. Write about a poor artist selling a painting to a rich patron.

70. Write about a famous guitarist who is developing arthritis in their hands.

71. Write about an event in King Kong's life from his perspective.

72. Write about the first Amish president of the US.

73. Write about a character's decision to shave their head.

74. Write about a character's new tattoo.

75. Write about a character visiting the state fair.

76. Write about a character getting chewing gum out of a cat's fur.

77. Write about a character accidentally getting locked in a wine shop all night.

78. Write about a character's first visit to an indoor gun range.

79. Write about a televangelist seeing a flying saucer hovering in his backyard.

80. Write about a character cooking over a campfire.

81. Write about a woman at the art museum who sees a 1600's Dutch painting that looks just like her.

82. Write about a character that can read another's mind while they shake hands.

83. Write about an old man's first visit to a yoga class.

84. Write about a character who abandoned their life to open a book shop in Algeria.

85. Write about a homeless character who has scraped up enough money to get halfway home.

86. Write about a hippie couple that drives a VW bus around to festivals and sells handmade goods.

87. Write something that comes to mind after reading this: "I'm half living my life between reality and fantasy at all times." -Lady Gaga

88. Write about a character's first class flight to Paris.

89. Write about a famous actor who returns home for
Thanksgiving for the first time in years.

90. Write about a character that makes wooden furniture.

91. Write about the picture on page 1.

92. Write about a character riding a bicycle at night.

93. Write about a stranger who hands a character an umbrella
then walks off in the rain.

94. Write about your elementary school from the custodian's
perspective.

95. Write about sleeping with the window open.

96. Write about a character being asked directions by a visitor
who speaks a foreign language.

97. Write about a character riding as the only passenger on a
city bus.

98. Write about a retiring person's last day on the job.

99. Write about a character finding a sealed pot of ink.

100.   Write about a character taking part in a charity walk.

101.   Write about a germaphobe who loses their hand
sanitizer at the airport.

102.   Write about a death-row inmate thinking about what to pick for their last meal.

103.   Write about a new teacher's first day teaching First Grade.

104.   Write about a mom's weekend when her ex-husband has taken the kids on a trip.

105.   Write a sonnet about winter.

106.   Write about a ten-year-old on Christmas morning.

107.   Write about an alien meeting a human from the alien's perspective.

108.   Write about an aging TV personality who is being courted by an extremist dictator.

109.   Write about an avid jogger who has a cold.

110.   Write something that comes to mind after reading this: "Attention to health is life's greatest hindrance." -Plato

111.   Write about someone who hears a strange noise outside their tent while camping.

112.   Write about a newlywed who must change into the opposite sex whenever the moon is full.

113.   Write about a character who attends their child's school play.

114.   Write about the image below:

115.   Write about a character that sees a televised police
    sketch and believes it is their next door neighbor.

116.   Write about a character trapped in traffic on their way
    to a crucial job interview.

117.   Write about a character with a breathing problem who
    is able to breathe easy for the first time in their life after
    going to the desert.

118.   Write about the first person who ate an oyster.

119.   Write about a character seeing their crush in a bathing
    suit.

120.   Write about a homophobe who accidentally falls in with a crowd of gay protesters.

121.   Write something that comes to mind after reading this: "As you simplify your life, the laws of the universe will be simpler; solitude will not be solitude, poverty will not be poverty, nor weakness weakness." -Henry David Thoreau

122.   Write about a hiker chased up a tree by a wild boar.

123.   Write about a character finding a book at the library written by their ex.

124.   Write about a character getting a wrong-number call for the suicide hotline.

125.   Write about a character standing in a long line at the department of motor vehicles.

126.   Write about a character sitting in a boring meeting or classroom.

127.   Write about a character who is making an elaborate meal for an important occasion, and they spill all of a critical ingredient.

128.   Write about a character that always follows the rules.

129.   Write about a character who is into Live Action Role Playing.

130.   Write about a character changing a flat tire on a busy street.

131.   Write a page of rhyming ABC's suitable for a parent to read to a young child.

132.   Write about a character by using this starting sentence: "The wind had finally died down; when I looked outside, I was shocked to see the massive bulk of an ancient oak had crashed across my car."

133.   Write about a 21-year-old character drinking alcohol for the first time.

134.   Write about a blind person shopping for a stereo system from the sales clerk's perspective.

135.   Write about a character who discovers their toilet is overflowing.

136.   Write about a group of friends who are trying to organize a movie night.

137.   Write about a board game for conservative right-wing voters.

138.   Write about a character that gets to meet their lifelong hero.

139.   Write about a character walking in their neighborhood at night who is confronted by a coyote.

140.   Write about a character who is visited by the police because their neighbor complained about loud music.

141.   Write about a character who calls the police because their neighbor plays loud music.

142.   Write about a character who wins the lottery.

143.   Write about a character who can grant one wish to anyone on January 1 of each year.

144.   Write something that comes to mind after reading this: "Many men go fishing all of their lives without knowing that it is not fish they are after." -Henry David Thoreau

145.   Write about a character hiking a well-defined trail in the woods, then the trail dwindles and ends.

146.   Write about a character that hears tiny screams when a flower is plucked.

147.   Write about a character who is performing a repetitive task for two hours.

148.   Write about a character finding a dead grandparent's musical instrument.

149.   Write about a character from the tropics who moves to another country and sees snow for the first time.

150.   Write about a character who attends a pottery class.

151.   Write about a character who suddenly starts hearing words hidden within bird songs.

152.   Write about a character who has a new work supervisor who is young and inexperienced.

153.   Write about a character who is asked to identify a body at the city morgue.

154.   Write about a character who is donating blood.

155.   Write about being at home during a power outage.

156.   Write about a character who goes to a vintage clothing shop.

157.   Write about a sculptor whose pieces come to life on Halloween night.

158.   Write about a radio astronomer who first detects an unmistakable alien signal.

159.   Write about a cab driver who picks up a movie star whose limo broke down.

160.   Write something that comes to mind after reading this: "Let us always meet each other with smile, for the smile is the beginning of love." -Mother Teresa

161.   Write about a character from a rural town who won a free cruise.

162.   Write about a character paddling a canoe against the wind on a wide lake.

163.   Write about a backwoods camping trip where a raccoon chewed up the only roll of toilet paper.

164.   Write about an employee that secretly lowers the boss's chair a quarter inch each day after the boss leaves.

165.   Write about a character that finds a huge hornet's nest in a tree near their front door.

166.   Write about a taxidermist who is trying to think up a clever business name.

167.   Write about a librarian that falls in love with a bounty hunter.

168.   Write about a ten-year-old that discovers a rusty pistol in some bushes at school.

169.   Write about a character buying a dog or cat at the animal shelter.

170.   Write about a character cleaning up election signs the day after their candidate lost.

171.   Write about two neighbors who compete with yard art.

172.   Write about a hypochondriac whose pinky suddenly starts twitching at random times.

173.   Write about a character trying to get their paintings displayed at a local bistro.

174.   Write about a kid whose babysitter let them watch their first scary movie.

175.   Write about a character seeing a hot air balloon drift over their house.

176.   Write about a parent and child making a time capsule.

177.   Write about a new homeowner's visit to the hardware store.

178.   Write about three adult siblings who have to clean out their childhood home after their last parent dies.

179.   Write about a senior citizen who goes to get a hearing test against their wishes.

180.   Write about a driver stopped by a slow-moving train.

181.   Write about a character in the near future who has a genetically-modified miniature elephant as a pet.

182.   Write about an amputee that is getting an improved prosthetic.

183.   Write about a character donating their broke-down car to a charity.

184.   Write about a character that gets a Christmas bonus at work.

185.   Write about a character finding a map from the 1800's with a mysterious 'X' on a spot near the local high school's

baseball field.

186.   Write about a character whose parent uses words inconsistently because of a stroke.

187.   Write something that comes to mind after reading this: "Zen is a liberation from time. For if we open our eyes and see clearly, it becomes obvious that there is no other time than this instant, and that the past and the future are abstractions without any concrete reality." -Alan Watts

188.   Write about a character carpooling to work with the philosopher Plato.

189.   Write about a character addicted to their noise-cancelling headphones, then the batteries die.

190.   Write about a character who is frying a turkey for a gathering with their new love's family.

191.   Write about a toddler throwing a huge tantrum in a grocery store.

192.   Write about a character that uses different fake foreign accents to mess with telemarketers every time they call.

193.   Write about a character who is a revolutionary war reenactor.

194.   Write about an old computer programmer who gets "down-sized," but the boss calls a month later, saying the old programmer is the only one who understands some crucial piece of old logic in their flagship product.

195.   Write about a late-night DJ at a small radio station in a small town.

196.   Write about a deadly disease outbreak that requires everyone to stay in their homes for 14 days.

197.   Write about a day in the life of a mail carrier on a lunar colony.

198.   Write about a first-century Roman who sells snacks at the coliseum during gladiator fights.

199.   Write about a character who is a modern hermit.

200.   Write about what happens after the last gasoline-powered automobile rolls off the assembly line.

201.   Write a poem that is inspired by these words (you are not required to use the words themselves):
Wake, Impress, Drop, Conflict, Rent

202.   Write about a small-time crook who gets called into an IRS audit.

203.   Write about the only straight person at their gay friend's party.

204.   Write about a child's first time going down the town's biggest hill in their sled.

205.   Write about a circus performer with a pet monkey.

206.	Write about a character's ex-convict uncle coming over to help repair the roof.

207.	Write about a substitute teacher who was not told about the planned fire drill.

208.	Write about a party with a bonfire on the beach.

209.	Write about a character who has a romance with someone who turns out to be a professional gambler.

210.	Write about a week-long wilderness trek where an outfitter has paired each hiker with a llama to carry the load.

211.	Write about a character who delivers legal cannabis products to people who order online.

212.	Write about characters who goes back in time to "rescue" breeding pairs of extinct ice age animals.

213.	Write something that comes to mind after reading this: "When you're drowning, you don't say 'I would be incredibly pleased if someone would have the foresight to notice me drowning and come and help me,' you just scream." -John Lennon

214.	Write about a character who is unexpectedly promoted after their boss is fired.

215.	Write about a time that you personally felt great fear.

216.   Write about a mysterious character that sells copper rings on the sidewalk.

217.   Write about snuggling with your favorite animal.

218.   Write about a beekeeper who sells honey at the local farmers market..

219.   Write about a character that runs away from home.

220.   Write about a character who has to transport a human heart in a cooler in their car.

221.   Write about a cake shop that loses power for a day.

222.   Write about a character who is a school tutor for young movie stars while on set.

223.   Write about a character in a belly dancing class.

224.   Write about a rich city person visiting an alpaca farmer to decide if they want to buy their own farm.

225.   Write about a present-day character who makes arrowheads.

226.   Write about a day in the life of a nicotine-starved school bus driver.

227.   Write something that comes to mind after reading this: "I have learned silence from the talkative, toleration from the intolerant, and kindness from the unkind; yet, strange, I am ungrateful to those teachers." -Khalil Gibran

228. Write about a female business executive stuck in an elevator with the building's maintenance man.

229. Write about a character that drives cars from an auction yard to a dealership 250 miles away.

230. Write about a character trying to make a business deal while struggling through morning rush hour traffic.

231. Write about a character that mentors a young person.

232. Write about a character that is mentored by an old person.

233. Write about a character by using this starting sentence: "He looked down from the roof, broom gripped in a suddenly shaky hand, at his ladder laying on the brown Autumn grass."

234. Write about a character waiting in traffic court to dispute a citation.

235. Write about a character voting for the first time.

236. Write about a character standing at the top of the high-dive for the first time.

237. Write about a character's 30th birthday.

238. Write about a character that runs a mobile pet grooming van.

239.   Write about a character who is visiting a physical therapist.

240.   Write about a jacket that has been passed through several generations of characters.

241.   Write about a character giving out candy on Halloween night.

242.   Write about a character who loses power and has to login for a day at a public wi-fi location.

243.   Write about a family holiday party where someone accidentally brings the wrong brownies - the ones containing cannabis.

244.   Write about a patron at a bar who, every few minutes, notices guys dressed like mobsters come in and disappear into a back room.

245.   Write about a civilian in France during World War II who is driving a mile ahead of a German formation and removing or changing all the road signs.

246.   Write about a family who owns a citrus orchard who have to scramble to protect their trees from impending frost.

247.   Write about a studio custodian who cleans up visiting actors' dressing rooms.

248.   Write about a character who runs the scoreboard for little league games.

249.   Write about the image below:

250.   Write about a transvestite mayor of a town with 500 people.

251.   Write about a diabetic that has to learn to give themselves insulin shots.

252.   Write about a character who has 20 minutes to evacuate because of a wildfire.

253.   Write about a gardener that digs up a civil war belt buckle in their backyard.

254.   Write about a character who wins an online auction and receives a piece of historic memorabilia in the mail.

255.   Write about a character that teaches chair exercises at the senior center.

256.   Write about a character who hears news that an asteroid as big as a football field is going to hit the Earth within 24 hours, but no one knows where.

257.   Write about a character that works at a brewery.

258.   Write about a character that makes costumes for the local theater.

259.   Write about a character who wears the team's mascot costume at football games.

260.   Write about a character that places flags at the graves of veterans each midnight before Memorial Day.

261.   Write about a secret heiress that runs a convenience store and bait shop at the lake she secretly owns.

262.   Write about what happens the day after a massive solar storm knocks out most of the world's electronics.

263.   Write about a character with ten bird feeders in the backyard.

264.   Write about an old man who gets free coffee at the convenience store, and he thinks it's because of his flirting with the clerk.

265.   Write about a character who is trying to recycle an old TV.

266.   Write about a nosy homeowner watching a strangely-dressed new neighbor move in.

267.   Write about someone's first experience on a duck hunt.

268.   Write about someone who is going to be late to work, and they have already been reprimanded by the boss for

chronic lateness.

269.   Write about an old soldier that visits a battlefield many decades later.

270.   Write about a character who works on a huge cruise ship.

271.   Write about a character at the grand opening of their sandwich shop.

272.   Write about a gay character going to a church Christmas service for the first time in ten years.

273.   Write five sentences or paragraphs of any length that all begin with the words, "I remember…"

274.   Write about a character awakened at 2:00 AM by an argument in the apartment upstairs.

275.   Write about a character who helps a stranger, then recognizes it is a famous musician.

276.   Write about a character that inherits a circus wagon after the death of their eccentric aunt.

277.   Write something that comes to mind after reading this:
"Afoot and light-hearted I take to the open road,
Healthy, free, the world before me..."
-Walt Whitman, Song of the Open Road

278.   Write about a government worker whose only job is to determine the standardized names of new flavors.

279.   Write about a character who wins a grant to spend a week at an art colony.

280.   Write about a character who is the designated driver for a group of drunk friends.

281.   Write about a bald man who is meeting with a toupee consultant.

282.   Write about an online vendor whose idea goes viral, and they are slammed with orders.

283.   Write about a character's first day working at a funeral home.

284.   Write about a character that needs to borrow money from a friend.

285.   Write about a character attending their class reunion.

286.   Write about a character that accidentally leaves their door open long enough for a squirrel to get into the house.

287.   Write about a character hiking in the deep forest miles from civilization who comes upon a group performing a Wiccan ritual.

288.   Write about a character that briefly sees their aged grandfather shirtless.

289.   Write about a young city character who is sent to live with country relatives for summer break.

290.   Write about a character that is one of four nominees for a prestigious award.

291.   Write about a character on a cross-country European train trip.

292.   Write about a character who is cajoled by a friend into visiting a civil war battle reenactment.

293.   Write about a counselor called to an unfamiliar school to assist students with the principal's sudden death.

294.   Write three paragraphs featuring these three words: Brother, Snow, Peppermint.

295.   Write about a struggling small business where a rumor of job cuts has started circulating.

296.   Write about a character who refurbishes old cars for resell.

297.   Write about a character who starts a microbrewery.

298.   Write about a character whose only recreation is singing in the church choir.

299.   Write about a character in a future time when learning a language is as easy as resting in a tanning bed for 15 minutes.

300.   Write about a character that wakes up late one night and sees a ghostly figure standing at the edge of their yard.

301.   Write about a character with a kidney stone.

302.   Write about a character who moves to an Asian country for a one-year work assignment.

303.   Write about a character with the flu.

304.   Write about a soldier returning home after being deployed in a war zone.

305.   Write about a character who, after a few dates, snoops in the other's closet and finds a stuffed cat.

306.   Write about a character who notices an aging parent is starting to lose important memories.

307.   Write about a volunteer usher at a major professional sports playoff game.

308.   Write something that comes to mind after reading this: "People have a hard time letting go of their suffering. Out of a fear of the unknown, they prefer suffering that is familiar." -Thich Nhat Hanh

309.   Write about employees at a company dealing with a customer data breach.

310.   Write about the scene in a high school teacher's lounge in 1972.

311.   Write about a paleontologist who discovers a modern timex watch embedded within the stomach area of a dinosaur.

312.   Write about a character who revisits their favorite annual vacation spot a year after the death of their spouse.

313.   Write about a child's first visit to a day-long music festival.

314.   Write about a musician/actor/dancer sitting in the waiting room for an audition with a famous director.

315.   Write about some people in a small company town (population: 237) after the company announces it is closing.

316.   Write about a topic using these words or concepts: Forest, Nest, Smoke.

317.   Write about a manager interviewing a narcissistic candidate who thinks they are overqualified for the job.

318.   Write about an undercover reporter with a secret camera who is publicly shaming unscrupulous auto mechanics.

319.   Write about a future time when intelligent robots have replaced teachers.

320.   Write about a character who is adjusting to a tiny apartment in a big city.

321.   Write about a character sitting next to someone on an airplane who is wearing too much cologne/perfume.

322.   Write about a character that overhears a stranger talking on the phone saying, "I am sure she killed him."

323.   Write about a character who was once a track star in school who is now running away from a pursuing policeman.

324.   Write about a fantasy wizard/witch who is getting too old to collect the rare, sometimes guarded, components of their spells.

325.   Write about a character who learns they are adopted.

326.   Write about a grocery store manager who sees a monkey in the produce section eating an apple.

327.   Write about a character who receives a beat-up cardboard box that had been lost in the mail for years.

328.   Write about a character in a business meeting who is the only dissenting voice in a decision.

329.   Write about a character going back to college after retiring from a 30-year job.

330.   Write about an avid gardener that discovers an exotic plant growing wild in their elderly neighbor's yard.

331.   Write about a young character who discovers they can somehow hear certain people speak 10 seconds before they actually speak.

332.   Write about a character trying to learn how to change their car's engine oil by watching a video on their phone.

333.   Write about a character attending a masquerade ball.

334.   Write about a character marching for a cause when they find themselves mixed in with the opposing group of marchers.

335.   Write about someone decorating their sterile cubicle for an upcoming holiday.

336.   Write something that comes to mind after reading this: "Don't grieve. Anything you lose comes round in another form." -Rumi

337.   Write about a character who has a disabled older sibling.

338.   Write about a small town's mayor who is also the grave digger.

339.   Write about a character that trains assistance dogs.

340.   Write about a character having a sudden, gassy digestive malady at an important business meeting.

341.   Write about a character waiting in a long queue to exchange a gift; then they see the gift giver come in.

342.   Write about a character who hides in a closet with their dogs when they see a tornado coming.

343.   Write about a tutor who discovers that their pupil is super-smart but too bored to do the work.

344.   Write about a character in the far past whose village is dying from a disease.

345.   Write three paragraphs featuring these three words: Volleyball, Lake, Hotdogs.

346.   Write about a character stopped in a huge traffic jam during a blizzard.

347.   Write about a character who gets several sad "wrong number" text messages and decides to reach out to the stranger.

348.   Write about s character unable to decide what to do with their deceased parent's prosthetic leg.

349.   Write about a character walking through a city on a normal day who discovers they are being followed.

350.   Write about a character who encounters a version of themselves that is twenty years older.

351.   Write about a bus driver using a rider's point of view.

352.   Write from a bus driver's point of view about the familiar "regulars" they pick up each day.

353.   Write about a character who receives a party invitation from a stranger who "has heard about your work."

354.   Write about a character watching the cloud of ground hornets they have disturbed swarm all over their still-running lawn mower.

355.   Write about a future time when all dietary warnings can be ignored since all dietary-related diseases can be cured.

356.   Write something that comes to mind after reading this: Bob took a long drink and said, "I know what really happened."

357.   Write about a character watching a stranger in business attire walk down a busy sidewalk during rush hour; the stranger is wearing stilts.

358.   Write about a character traveling in a foreign city who hears two strangers speaking about the character's hometown as if they also lived there.

359.   Write about a pedestrian who walks alongside a parked car and sees the driver weeping.

360.   Write about a character who sees the town preacher shove an old man to the ground at a ball game.

361.   Write about a character remodeling an old house they recently purchased who tears open a wall and discovers a wooden box placed 30 years ago.

362.   Write about an artist who experiences their first week-long art retreat.

363.   Write about a character laid off from a big company
who is interviewing with a tiny startup.

364.   Write about a child at the playground.

365.   Write something that comes to mind after reading this:
"What's right is what's left if you do everything else
wrong." -Robin Williams

About the Author

Mick is a writer and father who is not allowed to buy his own clothes. His creative nonfiction, fiction, and poetry have appeared in numerous consumer magazines, newspapers, literary journals, and three books of poetry. He is a member of the Georgia Writers Registry, Gwinnett County Writers Guild, and founding member of the Snellville Writers Group. In 2018, he created a quarterly reading series to benefit the local food co-op. He lives with his wife and a dozen larcenous squirrels in Atlanta, GA.

More at www.MickeyKulp.com.

*"If thou wilt make a man happy, add not unto his riches
but take away from his desires." ~Epicurus*